MW00353554

Sanctuary, Vermont

Sanctuary, Vermont

poems

Laura Budofsky Wisniewski

Sanctuary, Vermont
Copyright © 2022 by Laura Budofsky Wisniewski
All rights reserved.

ISBN: 978-1-949039-33-7

Orison Books
PO Box 8385
Asheville, NC 28814
www.orisonbooks.com

Distributed to the trade by Itasca Books
952-223-8373 / orders@itascabooks.com

Cover photo taken in Bolton, Vermont. Photographer
unknown. Used courtesy of The Vermont Historical
Society.

Manufactured in the U.S.A.

ORISON
BOOKS

CONTENTS

To Lou and to the "third thing."

About Main Street. 450,000,000 B.C.E.

Before there was this,
cataclysm doled itself out
in slow drift,
driven by restlessness,
by wander-love
in sluggish push
in shear of earth sheaths.
Mountains thrust up, rough, east.
Flatlands spread out, sweet-soiled, west.

Our Main Street runs the fault line like a scar,
say some.

Then

Our Year Without Summer. 1816

Every month there was a frost.
Frozen birds fell rigid from the sky.
Shorn sheep perished where they stood.
The corn crop failed, as did the grain.
Even Mrs. Moore, who heretofore had put on airs,
bowed her head in thanks for hedgehog stew and nettles.

In June, when Prudence Lexter froze while fetching wood,
I took her seven children in, poor spindly dears.
They died, all but the oldest girl, when the sickness came.
It struck us like a drunkard's blow.
Boys took up spades to help George Franklin dig the graves,
but the stunned ground would not break.

That smooth-skinned Pastor, up from Boston,
blamed it on our sins,
on our youngsters stealing kisses
in the birches down by Black Plum Lake.
A God who wields his anger cold?
I do not hold to that.

I say we are a frail and faltering flock
cast out into this wilderness of rocks and wind.
The touch of skin to skin
is all we've got.
I'd rather praise the blood
than curse the heart.

The War of the Rebellion. 1864

Gerald Whitcomb gave my Frank
ten poor acres and two cows
to muster in his place.

I begged my Frank to decline,
but he said it was for me and our boy,
and for the milk.

Now our boy's departed.
My Frank's got but one leg,
and he's not right in his mind.

Every Market Day, year round,
Gerald Whitcomb promenades through Town
prouder than sunrise.

That man smiles at me
and tips his hat.

The Hanging of Daniel Farrow. 1871

How can I describe the evil impulse?
A viper coiling up an apple tree.
Or the twist they give a wild grape vine to crack it, to break it.

And neither Father's strap nor Maman's holy book, nor bitter
    ipecac
brought me any peace when the Thing came on me,
though the snap of the strap was some small comfort.

In my fifteenth year I took to the drink, living rough in Pine Hill
    Woods
where there were others, lost as I.
Once a boy put his coat on me as I lay almost senseless to this
    world.

Unceasingly, Satan sounded in my skull hissing, whispering
of the rich who lived on Buckthorn Hill,
high above my Father, bent at his plow
and oh the chafe of rage
that bade me pound the wooden door of William Whitcomb,
    Financier,
that ordered me to drive the rusty blade through flesh to bone.

I ran as far as Ferrisburgh
but the stink of William Whitcomb's blood stuck to me
and the dogs tracked me down.

Tell Father and Maman that I was rotten at the pulp, my soul
    awry.
Let death come soft and green as moss. Let Hell be just and
    silent.
Let evil burn evil away at last.

On my Marriage Prospects. 1888

In our nowhere town of hills and rocks and wood
there are hardly any black men not my blood.
But a woman's got to marry, so my Mama says.
Off to the city of Vergennes
to meet that Mr. Ballande, aged forty-one.
I told my Daddy, No, I will not wed
a bag of bones. I do not care
if he is blacker than obsidian.

My own sister Lilah, stuck
with Wagoner Degree. That sad face
could make the sunshine cry.
Or what of Hannah Lawrence
and the youngest Aube boy?
He's white as milk in snow.
You would not catch me with a man
whose people thought me low.

There is someone.
He's a porter at the Sanctuary Inn.
His skin is brown and gold like Autumn afternoons.
In his uniform he resurrects my soul.
My Daddy says he'll surely roll right out of town
the way he rolled right in.
Good Lord, I say there's more to life than Church and butter.
I've read poetry.
My daddy says he's seen the world.
He says it's cold.

Well, it's cold here, too,
and small as yesterday,
without love.

My Murder

Isaac Luhkman, Peddler. 1865–1893

Some men are meant to be murdered,
some to live. Life's funny.
That I should hop like a rabbit from the Russian wolf
and end up in America,
right into the fox's mouth.
In Russia, I shivered.
In America? The same.
A poor man's coat is thin
no matter the country he is in.

Some men are meant for greatness,
some for toil. God decides
and writes it in the Book.
In Russia, I read Torah
like a rabbi's son.
In America, I bore my burden
on my back. I was lofty
as a donkey, but, alas,
with softer feet.

Some men are meant to end their line,
some to spread their seed. Let's face it.
I was handsome. Should I say it? Well endowed.
In Russia when I walked to Synagogue
the girls stole glances up and down.
America? The same.
They held my thimbles tenderly.
They felt my threads.
They stroked my cloth, though it was plain.

But such lonely nights,

in rocky fields of corn,
beneath a faceless moon.
The barred owl's hoot
I understood. But the rivers
babbled in a foreign tongue
while I dreamed my dreams of love,
also of blintzes oozing cheese.

So it was until a stranger murdered me
for my riches. Riches. Ha.
A bolt of cotton, sixteen needles, bread,
a spool of thread, a pot,
seven bars of soap.
The soap he could have used.

That night I bled, white
in moonlight, far away from home
where Mama and my sisters
baked the Sabbath bread,
where my father, never one for words,
scowled silently in prayer:
Blessed be He oh Lord
while I, his only son,
lay alone, unburied.

All men are dust.
And so am I.
Why trick us into praise and love and awe,
oh Lord,
then torment us with toil and loss?
Why first illuminate the world
then snatch the light?

If not for spite,
then what?

At the Tears & Fears Café After the Great War. 1919

You want burnt bread
with an iron crust,
a carp's strafed head
on a broken plate, doves' gut,
angry meat bled
dry, whiskey that cuts
across your tongue to the dead
part. You want the scald, but

they bring you quiet, dark plums.
They bring sweet, cool cream.
They know why you've come.
They know what you've seen.
They can read it on your wrists.
They'll take you like this,
empty.

Peonies. 1924

In June the petals of Maman's white peonies
bloomed against the picket fence
spreading out like mirth unbidden,
like girls, dressed fancy, laughing over nothing.
So it seemed the year
the Klan sprang up like mushrooms after rain,
sudden, strange.

The night the Klan burnt down our picket fence
there was no moon.
The shouts woke me.
I'd never heard the sound of hate before
but I knew it
the way a horse knows fire.
The sight.
The pointed hoods thrown back
like ladies' bonnets on a windy day.
Their faces torch lit.
Among them, my own beau, Augustus Bannister.
His mother. His father, mad with drink.
I'd seen a wild dog's mouth twist like that.

   The peonies were gone.
   Maman let the charred ground lay.
   Papa slept with his rifle near.
   The Klan did that, like mold to hay.
   And my blossom days ended.
   Sometimes the corn's silk is gold
   while there's rot in the cob.
   It's the same with the world.
   And it's best to know.

The Great Flood. 1927

Here at the bend,
Pond Brook has overrun its banks.

A man in a thin black tie and high black boots
slogs from shack to shack warning us to seek high ground.

And you with your fine wife, your clean sons, your house
of high calm from which you can look down

from Buckthorn Hill, you see us, the swamp
of our town, the roads tracked out like tears

to the farmlands, some by now deep under water,
livestock bawling, drowning in rain,

rain that kills the air, leaving only itself,
more and more of itself.

I can smell your skin on the good quilt, feel
your baby swim hard in me

as if there were a river
that led all the way to the sea.

The Forced Sterilization of the Abenaki People.
1931

You dream that you wake
and then that you wake
but you dream.
The dream tapes your eyes,
blows fog in your mouth.
The dream draws a map
of your organs.
You dream a sorrowful feeling
like a birch leaf washed downstream.
You try to call out.
The dream's hand covers your mouth.
You dream that you wake, bleeding
sorrowful blood from your organs.
Your organs keep trying
to speak without mouths.
There is a map of the dream on your skin
like tracks, your body scraped
hollow.
Wasn't there a baby?
In the dream you hunt for a baby.

Listen.
Follow the deer tracks,
cut deep in the juniper snow.
The People are camped at Black Plum Lake.
You can make it in three days
if you break
the dream
open.

Mark on a Tree. 1936

My mother's white sleeves flapped
like doves' wings in wind.
My father lifted me
and I flew.
In Summer, wild raspberries,
thick cream,
crayfish in the dappled stream.
But a wild hail felled the field.

As we could not pay our debt
they bid my father out
to Franklin Whitcomb's farm.
My mother warned away to Jericho.
I to the Poor Farm.
Hard girls stole my bread there.
All night a woman screamed
Jesus help me, help me.

The yellow apples cling
though the leaves have dropped.
The naked branches gnarl
and bow down.
On this tree
I scratch my mark
before I'm gone.

My name is Ellen White.
My mother brushed my hair
and let me stroke the hen
and hold the smooth eggs.
The Overseer says
I am nothing.
But once my mother danced
and I danced with her.

A Talk by Margaret Beech, Retired Army Nurse

In April 1939
deep snow still lay on the ground.
When they brought electric
to our farm, I heard it first from Bob Laverne
whose father laid the line.
"You'd best run home" he said,
"before they send the current through
your pasture fence and electrify you."
I always feared that fence,
its metal claws.

> *Dachau 1945.*
> *The barbed wire was still live.*
> *Bodies stacked like cord wood.*
> *Living lying with the dead.*
> *We sorted them like eggs.*
> *I closed my eyes, breathed slow*
> *until a calm came over me*
> *like midnight after snowfall.*

But what I meant to say was
it was April 1939
snow still on the ground,
the daylight almost gone.
I was so excited.
There was our farmhouse, bright
as if the sun sat in my Mother's kitchen.
Light reflected off the frozen field.
Light turned my boots to white,
the pasture fence to silver.
I cried with the thrill of so much light
and I ran.
Everything was alive.

For Grades One Through Three, Hawk Hill Schoolhouse. 1952

Italicized text excerpted from the film "Duck and Cover," written by Raymond J. Mauer and released by the U.S. Civil Defense Administration.

Every one of us must remember to do the same thing.
      60 starlings lift at once darkening the window of this
      schoolroom.
We must be ready for a new danger, the Atomic Bomb.
First you have to know what happens when an atomic bomb explodes.
      To know the woodstove backdrafts when the north
      wind missiles straight down from Hawk Watch.
It will look like this,
a bright flash,
brighter than the sun,
brighter than anything you have ever seen.
      That broken line on Main was a night snake in a
      shower of day sparks.
If you are not ready,
it could hurt you in different ways.
      And when the auger took his arm it was an engine of
      anger.
It can knock down walls or break windows all over town.
The atomic bomb flash could burn you worse than a terrible sunburn.
      A blind God showed itself to Mrs. Burns, overtaking
      both her eyes.
First you duck, then you cover.
      Hay hides you, but thin tines will find solidity.
Betty is asking the teacher;
"How can we tell when the atomic bomb may explode?"
      How can we tell when we're dead?
Always remember,
the flash of an Atomic Bomb can come at any time.

The oiled smell of pine planks, the smell of myself curled.
The first thing we would know would be the flash.
There is no time to look around or wait.
Duck and cover and do it fast.

And now the birds' wings beat like a man's war dream.
You might be eating your lunch when the flash comes.
We will all have to be ready to take care of ourselves.

Oh, I know to use the North Star like a white hot lullaby.
Paul and Patty know this; Tony knows.
Duck and cover!
That a boy Tony!

When the teacher weeps her mouth wide, bees arrive
humming.
We must do the right thing
if the Atomic Bomb explodes.

I will ride the horse home, whispers real Patty, through it.
Older people will help us with what to do as they always do.

But there might not be any grownups when the bomb explodes.
A tight fern coiled in the forest flashes.
Then you are on your own.

I have seen a horse burn and gallop flames across the
pasture.

Susan Rowen Comes to Elsewhere Farm. 1966

Never mind what I left behind.
I love so many things here.
The fog's lift.
The way our white peacocks
parade before the pigs.
Marie's plaid shirt flapping
as she urges the splattered cows
back to the barn in evening.
I love the neon parrots.
The one-eyed emu.
The shiny shards of mirror
glittering in the Atrium.
The bantams' strutting and clucking
as if their eggs were gold.
The speckled mornings of milking.

Tonight Marie swims Turtle Pond in moonlight,
piercing its bright swath of quiet,
pulling her square body through it,
tacking tremulous light
to the blackness underneath
while I stand among the peacocks
and birds of paradise.

I love how the old fear
is a tiny pebble turned silver.

The Veteran's Wife. 1974

From the bolted door of the eye,
the one-legged march of the heart,
the flowered jungle of the lungs,
the gut with its creatures and cages,
his cells whisper.

In the caves and tunnels of his body
the past vibrates on the membranes of the present
so softly
that I must still
utterly
and hold my breath
to hear.

Bob Brown Recalls. 1982

I used to walk the thirteen miles from Starksboro
every Saturday to court my Bea.
Her tongue was sharp as a skinning blade
even then. Cut through
most anything.
Hands on hips, chin up
the way a girl who isn't pretty learns.
After I saw her beat the rugs in Spring
I'd toss my hat in first
before entering her kitchen.

Byron's moonshine still was down the road back then.
God, that stuff was rough.
Few things we had enough of.
Work. Had enough of that. Cows, too.
Nowadays, where's one young man
knows his way around a three-horse plow?
Not even my own boy,
up to Burlington with that heating-cooling outfit.

Keep thinking backward.
Sunday picnics down by Black Plum Lake.
Young ones running wild as turkeys.
Hot bread. Pork chops. Rhubarb berry pie.
Miss those days.
Smell of hay, cut new.
Bea.

After the Hostile Takeover. 1990

Far from New York City
in a field to the north of the river
a man met the gaze of a bobcat.

>He'd leveraged the surprise buyout
>with a seven figure blind pool
>gutting the last of the die-hards.

Between the man and the bobcat
an acre of switchback flared gold.
The hum of toil stilled.

>Soiled with the sweat of the boardroom
>dulled by the second martini
>he lost the heat of the kill.

The bobcat waited, crouching,
its ears flickering like thoughts.
The man was

>afraid of the shadows between things
>of the lift of hairs on his body
>of the ghost in the dew as it fell.

On September Eleventh, 2001

I watched a fledging robin on the narrow ledge
    crouching
        down
            into herself
then lengthening upward
from the backward curl of her refusing
    toes
        to the whirled
            tuft of her crown,
losing courage
    turning back toward
        the abandoned nest
            that had once been everything
and now was no more than a dead eye left open.

She gathered herself
    crying out like any child,
her next step
    impossible
        inexorable.

Caught in a sudden flare of sunlight
she seemed to be
    falling
        flailing
            her speckled wings
                flapping
                    scrambling for the uplift
                  failing
                    on fire.

Margaret Gadreau's Mike. 2007

Killed last March.
Afghanistan.
That boy could fix anything.
We heard she walked to the barn in her nightgown
let the chickens out
and lit it.

Pond Brook. 2011

From suppertime till breakfast it rained
without cease, in sheets.
The water rose and rose like rage.
Some of us rode out to the Farrow Farm
to help Bill Jackman get the herd to higher ground.

The little stream on West Plank Road
swelled triple-fold and hurled itself head first
like suicide. It split the Martins' house in two,
them watching from the knoll,
the children silent as Sunday.

That Wall Street guy,
who bought the Whitcombs' place with cash,
just before the crash that felled the small
and lifted up those too big to fail, even he,
paddling his shiny kayak,
rescued Lydia Delaney off her roof.
Now he knows what we already knew.
Lydia never has had the sense
to come in out of the rain.

Along Pond Brook, Two Pines Trailer Park
washed away. Just like that.
They never should have let that outfit
build again down there.

Mary Beecher rushed her daughter's insulin
to the Tears & Fears Café
to keep it cold until she got her power back,
the windows of the Tears & Fears
white with the breath of our town.
Andre cooked up a vat of barley soup.

Max put out a box.
You could throw a dollar in or not,
for the fields were fouled.
Machinery mud-choked.
Waterbury buried under water.
No one knew when the checks and food stamps
might be mailed again.
Ramona waltzed the floor, a pot of coffee in each hand
shouting insults without concern
for gender, class, or station.
This calmed us all.

The lowlands meet the hills at Main.
My mother used to say
If you are ever drowning, raise your eyes;
a rich man will be watching.
It's true. I've never seen a creek run uphill.
But I have seen a ripple spread
all the way to the border.

Now

Dawn. Sanctuary, Vermont

In snow as light as breath
the Dalai Lama's driver
jazzed on oolong tea and lack of sleep
prays in a long exhale
      as the tires skid
      then grip.

From the Mountain View Hotel
a woman in last night's clothes
nursing the last of the pack
watches the silver rental car
      almost lose
      the road.

In front of Aube's Quick Mart
a boy with a glowing shiner,
his brother's keys, and a cellphone
looks up in time to glimpse
      the slow slide through
      the light on Bridge and Main.

Just then, in Urgent Care
a man with a DNR
dreams that his first wife
is calling out his name
      from the heart rate
      monitor.

Every day has at least one marvelous thing.
Today it's the Dalai Lama smiling
at a sparrow stitching upward
      through the glitter
      of the sun-struck snow.

Behind the Green Hedge

Behind the green hedge
retired bankers play for dimes.

Along the green hedge
shattered soldiers stagger home.

Beyond the green hedge
angry children hurtle stones.

Pigeons startle, fill the air
like petals rising up

like ghosts and ashes
rising up.

To November Gods

Prayer to the god of chainsaws.
  Preserve my beloved's fingers.
  Let the notches in the standing wood break true.

Prayer to the god of dead leaves.
  Shelter the refugees.
  Hide them from wild-eyed dogs, from their
  masters.

Prayer to the god of caulking.
  Mend the breach
  through which our death insinuates.

Prayer to the god of supper.
  Bless the meaty stew
  that turns the rough cheek of snowfall.

Prayer to the god of thin light.
  Great is even the first pale ray
  breaking through.

Midnight Till Four

Tonight it's Kandahar:

The dream of the little girl
with two of his bullets in her.
Sometimes it's the arm
with a perfect hand attached.
Sometimes Bill Caldwell's face
silently blowing away.
Tonight it's Kandahar.

Dave Franklin walks up and down Main Street
every night from midnight till four.

At the Tears & Fears Café
the light in the kitchen is on.
Four am. Finally.
Max unlocks the door.
He takes a chair from the table.
Ramona sets Dave's place.
A cup, a plate, a teaspoon,
a bowl with packets of sugar,
cream in a miniature pitcher,
a menu that's always the same.
Every day except Monday,
blueberry pie and hot coffee,
Andre oiling the bread loaves,
Max writing out the day's specials,
Ramona folding the napkins'
wild white wings
while the eyes of the streetlights close slowly
and dawn kills the shadows on Main.

Amanda Rowe's Dream

I dreamed
vanda coerulea, eucalyptus, magnolia grandiflora
poked up through the snow.

Winter's so long and full of nothing,
men go soft in the lower forty.
TV's always on.

Last Saturday we had a thaw
and as I scraped the plates I saw
William eyeing me that way.

Good lord, I thought, maybe Spring is coming.
Sanguinaria canadensis blossomed in my blood.

It wasn't love, though,
but longing.

At the Assisted Living Facility

There is the photograph of her
between two men in open-collared shirts.
A leopard at their feet. There is an ocean,

a bridge, the War.
There is conquest and the satin sheet.
The little boy who died. The cello

wide between one's thighs.
There is a rosary and a mantra.
The corridor. Red wine. Blood.

There is the knife like a life
of the mind. The river mud.
The servants with their silver

trays. The scent of laundry soap.
There is rising at noon in the fawning
heat. The arduous voyage, the gasp

of delight at the white
sand beach. The waves' swell.
The tiny broken shell.

Max's Cure

When the SSRIs, MAOIs, Yoga, Zen,
and Cognitive Behavioral Therapy
turned their backs on Max,
the Spirits stepped in.

The Spirits worked nights,
breaking into his dreams without knocking.
using symbols of psychoanalysis,
especially tunnels and guns.
They showed up in kooky neckties, t-shirts from the
            sixties.
They lured Max down dead caverns,
through fields of dirt and shards
into black-out forests,
then leapt out from behind trees
farting.

One morning, Spring,
Max's frayed blanket floated.
Bloodroot blossomed.
The ground beat like a drum.
Snakes sunned themselves on his car's hood
spelling a message
from Them:
Ha ha ha, it read,
Gotcha.

In April

She left him, that arrogant bastard.
She was halfway over the Tappanzee
before she knew she'd never
miss their kitten,
never miss croissants,
never miss the *New York Times* Arts and Leisure Section.
She turned the GPS off in Ellenville, New York.

Spring was going backwards.
The leaves were nibs again.
In some nameless Vermont town,
with a green hedge along its main street,
at a neon sign announcing
The Tears & Fears Café,
she stopped

famished.
The host intoned the specials.
The cake was shaped like an angel.
The waitress unfurled her arms.
The chef made the sign for sky.
Outside forsythia and lilac
mistook the sun for heaven
and released their meditation
in an epiphany of petals.

ICE

My brother says, *It's bad.*
Snow, ice. Stay in Mexico.
But I come anyway.
Gadreau's dairy farm.
At least the double wide is warm.
An old guy, going home
mumbles, *Enough is enough,*
and gives me his boots
with rubber stars on the soles
for the ice.
Ice polishes the path to the barn.
Ice grows a skin on the pond.
Ice hangs from the roof
like wolf teeth, hard and glistening.

Fourteen-hour days, two milkings.
Every Saturday I drive with the guys to town
and every time, my brother says, *Stupid,*
don't go. Agents could be anywhere,
in the grocery, the hardware store.

Maybe he's right, maybe he's wrong,
but I go. I'm a man,
not an animal to be tethered,
to be milked.

Song of the Cash Register Associate

What do you know of me
Ms. All Organic Only, Gluten Free?
And Mr. Chips And Dip And Beer, don't
call me dear. Oh
you Skinny Girls,
you Diet Coke and Salad Greens,
not all is what it seems.

The night is mine.
I'll pour wine, dark and full.
I'll stir the soup, lick the spoon.
The hunger moon will move.
Love will come when it comes.
The waiting spreads like ice cream
melting on my tongue.

M. "Rif" Williams Plays the Tears & Fears Café

Rif
play that bone
your old lady says
     come home
but
the boys are in
     the zone
and the one-eyed jack
     in the back
is yelling
     lift me baby
lift me
     from my grave.

Do it.
Dig
those ghosts and angels
     up
then slay them
     death by bliss
transfiguration
breath complete

     bless
the blinded 5/4 beat
of sweet confabulation.

Here at the Tears & Fears Café.
Tonight only.
     The Small Still Voice Quintet.

2.

But now
with just one day left
    Rif's pump's thump
    echoed
just
    the IV drip
    tripped tempo
one day
    shift change
    flipped the mode
One day,
    one,
            just one day
left to
    live
and couldn't she
couldn't she just
    this one time
lay her big cool hand
    on his cheek,
    withered leaf of it,
just one
just one time
just one.
No.
But oh
it was the metal nights he'd loved
    not her
the shadows, scotch and blow
    not her,
the blind flight
    of the high notes
the gravel prayer
    of the snare

but oh
but now
just one
but,
      no.

     3.

The feathered blanket
    held
    him
    down
like a father's
    knuckled
       hand.
The rustling darkness
    held
    him
    down
like a mother's
    secret
       tear.
The thick air
    held
    him
    down
like a small child's
    silky
       ear.
Tongue
thumb
toes
held
him
down
then

the heart
        monitor
laid down the melody
and he took it
        wild and winged
took it up
        all him
up
        all bone
up
        and home
on the second sweetest note
he'd
        ever
                blown.

        4.

After,
she smoothed the white sheet
she touched the empty clothes.
Baby, she whispered, hand on his cheek,
        I had a soul, too.

From a Map of the Region

In the cave of the miscarried
I found a tiny bone
dry to my lip's skin, cool as afternoon.

In the meadow of last snakes
I found, for flaying, honed,
razor thin, a shard of stone.

On the precipice of endless wind
I found a feather, black as blood, worn down
shaft hollowed, sheen gone.

On the lake of recurring dreams
I found the sliced moon
shaking, sinking, stunned.
            This is what is meant by empty.

Elle Itoua Dreams

Ah, this small village
with her scrubbed churches, her loyal hedges,
her gardens, honeyed, cloying.
One walks the high street
choking on fumes
of severed grass and lilacs.

Here, the starry nights are cluttered
with creature cries and nonsense.
Wild dogs bark from boredom.
Raccoons rifle through rinds.
Frogs obsessed with love
chirp desperately till dawn.

I dream. Each night I dream
the fire, the smoke, the screams.
Each night my mother recedes
beautiful yet faceless,
and I call to her, my arms reaching out in the dark.
Always my own cries wake me.

If even the graveyards are deaf,
where does one go?
My true village is shattered.

At the Assisted Living Facility (2)

When the window opens,
when the light's eye opens,
I will leave you,
leave the dishes in the sink,
the silver forks,
the crumpled sheets, your skin.
I will leave
the orchard of black plums.
I will not recall
that hotel, broken down,
nor that day of waves
and rampant wind,
nor the ravens' call
nor your skin.
When it opens again.

My Husband Doesn't Talk About the War

Deadfalls in the dark.
Fault lines in the dream.

In everybody's dreams hands
bleed. In everybody's hands the knife edge
gleams. In everybody's wound salt
sings. The seam closes
quickly, jagged.

Thunder in the stones.
Comets whistling down.

Everybody wakes
for second watch. Everybody's trembling fingers
touch the sleeping child. Everybody's touch
burns. The gaping night's singed
shut with cigarettes.

Lightning in the canopy.
Flares of ghostly lilies.

In everybody's throat words
die. In everybody's words death
hides. Everybody's silence sets
the orphaned child on fire. Tell me
my darling. Whisper it. In the dark.

Splitting Wood. Veterans Day

Only half the deadwood's down.

A man's maul releases
the sour smell of poplar,
severs the gnarled scars of oak,
bites through yellow birch.

The sun lies low.
There is a dangerous dusk
in which old shadows walk
the mined perimeter.

Twenty-eight nights fall
between one full moon and the next.
The delicate skulls of birds and snakes
are hidden in dead leaves.

It's not the lost leg,
not the dreams
that strip the man out.
It's the children.
Their open eyes.
The waste.

I Imagine You in the Workshop

I imagine you in the workshop
a mile and a half from the cabin
you built for Marie and the children
when it was only beer and pills.

I imagine the smell of sawdust
the leather of your armchair
the tools above the work bench
hung properly from nails.

I imagine the forty-four,
the simple click of the hammer,
the metal of the muzzle
cold against your temple,
          your finger on the trigger
          bent at the first knuckle.

Like when you hit that ten-point buck
but missed the heart.
You tracked him by the blood trail.
He stared directly at you
while you took him with one to the head.
No struggle.

I remember you telling that story
when it was only beer and pills.

After Watching That Show on DNA and Race

I mentioned it to Phil. He closed
one eye, a red-zone-warning sign.
In his crushed-glass voice

he said, *If that was you*
had that blood, I'd a never
married you. It took a beat

to hit.
I spun up inside myself,
like feathers in a dryer,

then floated down,
but not into the same old
what-do-I-know shoes.

I'm ashamed to remember,
that time in the parking lot of Harding's Hardware
Phil swerved his size-matters Chevy

right at a black lady and her baby.
I just sat there, my soul on pause,
sin-silent, texting my sister.

After the Divorce

I shook the tablecloth until
      a rat
      chased the crumbs,
      crossed the portal,
      landed hard.
My god,
      his tread was like a man's
      and when he walked the piano keys at midnight
he played jazz like Monk.
How he loved bananas.

Through those graying evenings I
      ate cheap chocolate
      googled "rat"
      and cried
while he,
      just the other side of sheetrock,
gnawed the walls away.

Why did I wait so long to take him down?

The day I bought the trap from Harding's Hardware,
      Mr. Harding warned me
      not to break a hand
yet who was there but me
      to pry the cold steel jaws?
A believer would have prayed.
How could I sleep?
Yet I did.

By breakfast he was dead alright,
      grown fat on my fruit,
      stretched prostrate at the trash can's feet.

Now
when the visions visit me
     like spiders hung from heaven
     spinning tongues of light
     as if to shape the names of days or children
     who will testify?

No one—
     I have slain the witness.

Her Story

She told me,
don't make
black and white photography
of the blood fear I feel
for my child's black body
in this tight white town.
Don't take my story
for your poetry.

She told me,
you can say my mother was born right here
on Butter Hill.
Say she taught me how to conjure
an orchid from a sodden log,
how to dig deep down for a taproot.
You can say my son is my heart,
my orchids are my glory.

Diary. November 2016

Entry 1

Last night, no sleep.
The coy dogs' howls, the barred owl's screech, the fox's
    scream,
the cries of their prey.

Entry 2

The train dream again.
People on the platform always turn away.
I can't move my legs.

Entry 3

Swastikas. Today I rifled through my little cedar box
with the broken lock. I found it, my tiny Star of David.
A woman in the canned goods aisle said this country
    needs a purge.

Entry 4

Dawn. The Parsons' field. The snow geese have flown.
Will I know when to call the children in?
When to go?

What Ramona Knows

There is a place
where they kill almost everyone eventually.
In such a place there is always
the sorting of people into different queues.

Yet in this same place
clear mountain streams run
over flat black stones with thin white lines.

Here, a certain kind of bird,
small and grey with a yellow beak,
is common.
The bird will eat striped sunflower seeds
right from the hands of the old.
This is a place where even a grandfather is killed,
perhaps for writing in a tattered book
or for drinking sweet tea in the back of a café.

When They come,
he closes his eyes and turns his palms toward the clouds
as if to ask:
what can you really take from me?

Or as if he is inviting
a flock of common birds
to carry him away.

Ventilator Policy at Plum Lake Clinic. 2020

A veined hand shows.
Doctor Lin says: *Too old.*
She thinks: *Not enough life years.*
How many light years?
These are questions for astronomers.
She reads the next chart on the screen.
She says: *Young. Strong heart. We'll vent him.*
Doctor Lin's legs are heavy
as if this is a planet
with double gravity.
She thinks: *I miss my grandmother*
who is a lustrous heavenly body now in long orbit around a
             distant star.
She thinks: *Better than here.*
Given the policy.

The Difference Between a Year and a Lifetime

For a year you can exalt in a feather,
for a year you can forget what hit you,
forget the blade that cut through
the turpentine of mango.
For a year you can plan the party
you will throw when the year is over
or plan an assignation
at the corner of time and jasmine.
For a year you can read the headlines,
feed the sparrow,
listen for wingbeats just out of earshot,
beat the ground for earthworms,
excavate the dreams
you dreamed the year before.
For a year you can be lonely
as pajamas in the daytime, lonely
as the doorknob, lonely
as the threshold, lonely
as the light shaft
on the polished wooden floor.
You can do it for a year.
A year is just a door
you are slowly walking through,
but a lifetime is this window,
its eye,
that sky,
this wind.

Our Love is as Old

Our love is as old
        as your shoes,
the ones that died
        last October,
the soles
        splitting almost in two
on that awful walk on
        the North road that ended
with you whistling Stardust
        and me
muttering under
        my breath
while above us the leaves were igniting
        as if they were tiny new planets.

Our love is as old as
        the red couch
with its two asymmetric depressions:
        a crater created by your ass,
        an amphitheater from mine,
the red
        a flamboyant example
of the triumph of whim over wisdom,
        for it sits
        in the den
        like a dazed rose
in a patch of onions and gravel.

Our love is as old as that
        old joke
where they only eat half the chicken,
old as that
        recurring dream

where I have to teach class in pajamas,
as old
     as your glory-day story
about hitchhiking
     through North Dakota and the time
     that scary-eyed trucker
     held a fifth of Bourbon in one hand
     and spun
     the wheel with the other,
the sky so splattered with diamonds
     it was as if you'd never seen night
     until he pulled the rig over
and left you on route 69.

Oh,
our old,
old
love
forgets where the bones have been buried,
     suns itself on the back porch,
     shifts its haunches a little,
     sighs with satisfaction
while yellow leaves drop with exhaustion
     and goldenrod
     perfumes the air.

The Tears & Fears Café Offers Curbside Pick-up

Dear loyal patrons,
Remember our sign's neon halo,
our ancient tables
with their fork-etched
names, Ramona's voice
putting the whole town
in its place, and the way
our hard days turned to din then song?

Dear loyal patrons,
Remember Andre's Grief Soup,
its lemon a narrow stairway
to a tiny upstairs window,
Max's One-sided Noodles,
how they swam
in a sea of saffron like the past
swims in tenuous laughter,
how they dyed
the town's tongues yellow,
and Ramona's Cake of Sundays
shy as a dove in springtime,
restless at the first bite
but then fluttering its wings?

Eat. Drink.
Tonight let the clink of the town's
spoons sound
in the unsure air.

*

Plum Lake Rural Clinic #10. 2061

"O viriditas digiti Dei" / "O greenness of God's finger"
                    –*Symphonia*, Hildegaarde von Bingen

Still half asleep, three young physicians follow Sister
        Jessica.
Sister's God thinks in greens and threes: creation, fall,
        salvation.
She says, *Do not obstruct God's genesis of leafy wings.*

She says, passing between pallets,
In all creatures, there is viriditas. In all dirt, viriditas.
In all souls, those green-tongued bells, there is viriditas.

Surely, the tender shoots that crack the sodden walls,
the pale pink skin that closes the wounds' eyes,
noon's breakthrough rays, testify to it.

Sister, like a blade of grass in wind,
tends the sick, bending over them
then straightening to listen to God's strain,

while in the Courtyard of the Drowned, nurses sing
the Lithianium. Tame rats doze
in crabgrass and St. John's Wort. What comfort those
        voices are.

The old machines: IV, X-Ray, EKG, lie
moldering in Storage Closet One.
Do not mistake the relic for the spirit of the Saint,

says Sister Jessica. *Seas recede, seeds redress last breaths*
with green. Do not obstruct God's urge
to lick clean the afterbirth.

NOTES

In "Peonies," the speaker is of French Canadian descent and Catholic. The K.K.K. gained a foothold briefly in Vermont in the mid 1920s. Most K.K.K. activities were aimed at immigrants and Catholics, though their targets included all non-white, non-Protestant Vermonters. ("The K.K.K. in Vermont, 1924." Vermont Historical Society, vermonthistory.org)

"A Talk by Margaret Beech, Retired Army Nurse" is inspired by a taped interview with Gussie Lavern in which she reflects on her past, including the day electricity came to her family's farm. ("Community Voices: The story of Hinesburg's Gussie Levern, born in 1918." *The Hinesburg Record*)

ACKNOWLEDGMENTS

Thank you to the following journals for first publishing some poems in this collection.

Alternating Current: "After the Hostile Takeover. 1990"

American Journal of Poetry: "Mark on a Tree. 1936"

Blueline: "From a Map of the Region" (as "Four Empty Worlds")

Hunger Mountain Review: "Splitting Wood. Veterans Day"

Passengers Journal: "Margaret Gadreau's Mike"

Ruminate Magazine: "The Difference Between a Year and a Lifetime" (winner of The 2020 Janet B. McCabe Poetry Prize)

Saranac Review: "What Ramona Knows" (as "There Is")

Thank you to my beloved, Lou Colasanti, for his invaluable feedback, his unwavering and loving support, and his enthusiasm for this book. I could have never seen it through without him.

Thank you to editor Caroline Shea for her light touch and x-ray vision, to Jeff Volzer for his always helpful comments, to dear friends Sue Jacobs, Jill Mackler, and Linda Smith for actually wanting to read the manuscript, and for believing in it.

Thank you to Orison publisher and editor, Luke Hankins, for seeing the "spiritual perspective" in this book and for his respectful, astute, no-nonsense editing.

Thank you to Katie Ford, Maurice Manning, Betsy Sholl, and Mary Jane Dickerson for their generous, careful reading of the manuscript and for their very kind endorsements.

ABOUT THE AUTHOR

Laura Budofsky Wisniewski is the author of the chapbook *How to Prepare Bear* (Redbird Chapbooks, 2019). Her work has appeared or is forthcoming in *Image, Hunger Mountain Review, Ruminate, Saranac Review, Confrontation,* and other journals. She is winner of The 2020 Janet B. McCabe Poetry Prize, The 2019 *Poetry International* Prize, and The 2014 *Passager* Poetry Prize. She lives and writes in a small town in Vermont.

ABOUT ORISON BOOKS

Orison Books is a 501(c)3 non-profit literary press focused on the life of the spirit from a broad and inclusive range of perspectives. We seek to publish books of exceptional poetry, fiction, and non-fiction from perspectives spanning the spectrum of spiritual and religious thought, ethnicity, gender identity, and sexual orientation.

As a non-profit literary press, Orison Books depends on the support of donors. To find out more about our mission and our books, or to make a donation, please visit www.orisonbooks.com.

For information about supporting upcoming Orison Books titles, please visit www.orisonbooks.com/donate, or write to Luke Hankins at editor@orisonbooks.com.